15 STEPS TO
TEAM SUCCESS

15 Steps to Team Success

LEARN HOW TO RUN ANY TEAM
LIKE A WELL-OILED MACHINE

RJ Wolfe

ISBN: 154324680X
ISBN 13: 9781543246803
Library of Congress Control Number: 2017905549
CreateSpace Independent Publishing Platform
North Charleston, South Carolina

For the leaders of today and tomorrow...

ACKNOWLEDGEMENTS

I originally wrote *15 Steps to Team Success* in 2009. My work with the Landmark Forum® in 2017 helped shape this rewrite to deliver a more powerful and authentic message that I hope will move and inspire all who read it. A great many thanks to everyone who contributed to the success of this edition, and I especially would like to thank Jeff Willmore, Avanish Aggarwal, Mark Lasoff, Greg Kilgore, Edward Dooley, Rich Crabtree, Rosie O. Vazquez, Eyca Moticska, Guita Kurd, and Louis LeBrun for their steady insights into creating a life in action which remains powerfully in action. My deepest gratitude goes to my wife Jurate L. Wolfe for introducing me to the world of Landmark.

TABLE OF CONTENTS

CHAPTER 1

GETTING STARTED

Teamwork is one of those intangible business tools that is regularly overlooked as a vital component to the overall health and success of a business. The bottom line is: you can't do it alone. Without your team in place doing what it is supposed to do, there is no business. This is simply a point of fact. Mastering the ability to nurture and integrate a culture of teamwork in your business will turn an intangible business tool into an imperative driver of your success.

Congratulations on purchasing this concise handbook. You have taken the initial step in building a successful, productive, trustworthy, loyal, profitable, and enthusiastic team. By following the format I outline here, you will see results immediately. With each new step you employ, you will see an improved connection with your team.

Let's take a look at why the problem happens in the first place. You may be surprised to know that the problem doesn't necessarily stem from your team members.

Why the Problem Happens

Poor teamwork can be reduced to five main components. Without being addressed, each of these components branches out into other elements. Each new element becomes more destructive when stacked atop the last.

A lack of trust among team members gets in the way of effective team management. Teams that perform extraordinarily well have a high degree of integrity and trust among their teammates. Top performers do what they say they are going to do, and team members trust one another to move their action items forward.

Insufficient motivation is another component of poor teamwork. People are naturally willing to sacrifice happiness and mental health for the knowledge that they'll have a job tomorrow. Keeping a job is only temporary motivation. Simply having job security is not enough to maintain joy and teamwork among your ranks. This book will show you how to manage these expectations and motivate people beyond mere job security. You will move and inspire them to move powerfully into action and to remain powerfully in action. In return, you will develop a fun and productive workplace.

People are, by virtue, *reluctant to change*, no matter whether it is the color of their work socks to the routines they subject themselves to in meeting project deadlines. The concept of change to many people is a source of fear and results in poor teamwork.

Lack of accountability is disastrous to a strong functioning team. Consider this, if I told you I were going to bring you some chicken soup tomorrow so you can get over your cold faster but didn't show up, how would you feel? If I got away with making a promise but not delivering, how inclined will I be to follow through on future promises I make to you? How inclined would you be to believe me?

The same is true for the workplace. If members of your team can make promises to deliver and then not deliver, everyone suffers. The proverbial cold, as I illustrated above, will continue. Everyone will get sick, nobody will feel any obligation to follow through on their word, and nothing will get done. Productivity will come to an abrupt, screeching halt. Holding everyone accountable, including yourself, is a vital element of team success.

Finally, our own worst enemy is ourselves. *Failure to clearly communicate the expectations* you have of each individual member of your team to each individual member of your team will eventually result in the failure of the team. Once everyone knows what they are supposed to be doing, the benefits of communication are made evident. There will be nothing to hold your team members back from pulling their own weight and lending a helping hand as often as necessary to each other from the start of a project to the finish.

In this book, I have included some methods to help you clearly communicate your expectations and plant the seeds for a highly effective, productive, and trusting team. A team that is open to embracing change and accomplishing common objectives.

I have broken down this manual into fifteen separate and concise steps. When you see "**TAKE ACTION**" in capital and bold letters, it means stop reading and complete the step. *15 Steps to Team Success* is designed to align you with success as you move through the handbook. It may be helpful to read through the entire contents of this book once before taking any action. It is imperative however to read it through a second time and actually act as you proceed through the chapters.

CHAPTER 2

STEP ONE—FIRST THINGS FIRST

TAKE ACTION: Make time. Create a comprehensive list of things you are struggling with or wish to improve upon. Then outline the areas of deficiency within your team's cohesion and effectiveness.**

Go over this outline several times with people outside the workplace to tone down possible harsh undercurrents stemming from your dissatisfaction with your team's performance. **You want to stick to the facts, not overshadow your main points with obscure emotional undertones. You should remove emotions entirely from your analysis.** Some points to consider are the actual dollar costs in terms of lost time, lost productivity, and missed opportunities.

It is also a good idea to list the personal costs to you as the manager for nonperformance of your goals and objectives. These include frustration, burnout, lost personal opportunity, and possible termination or unprofitable business.

First, identify how, by action, inaction, or both, you have been a part of the problem rather than the solution. Further convey to your team where you personally have room for improvement. They will appreciate you for being genuine with them. **Important: Do not communicate these points to the team until you are prompted to do so in this handbook (Step Ten-The Change Meeting).**

Ninety percent of businesses fail because of poor management decisions and failure to plan. Much of this statistic stems from the inaction or failure of a manager, CEO, entrepreneur, or group leader to be honest with himself or herself about what their goals are and where they need improvement in his or her management style.

By failing to plan and not clearly aligning your goals with your team, your team members will get confused. There will not be a united vision to work toward. Your team will find itself doing work, but to what end? While each of these consequences may be overcome one at a time - when they are combined - the result is team stress, team fractures, and eventually team collapse.

You should not develop a plan just for plan's sake. Some organizations go through the motions of developing a plan simply because common precedent dictates that every good organization must have a plan, any plan.

Don't do this. Like most everything in life, you get out of a plan what you put into it. Please take the time to make your outline above - but don't just do it - do it right. And the only way to do it right is to be honest with yourself about your own truths and your own myths.

A second limitation leaders often face is not understanding their environment. Not fully understanding your environment hinders results. Always remember that you are a productive manager. Production requires constant awareness of changes and advances that facilitate productivity. These changes and advances in turn create the potential for greater results.

After you fully understand your environment you can set meaningful priorities. Properly arrange your priorities and keep pace with your industry's changing dynamic. Doing this consistently will lead you to positive results.

Third, your own personal well-being can also be a priority. Burnout, frustration, lost personal opportunities, and termination are all real possible outcomes for you. It is okay to admit to yourself that one of your priorities is your health or career as a professional and manager. This can only be a priority, however, if you hold the same belief of your employees and team members. Their well-being, their health, their job security, and their career success must be a priority for you too.

Once you've identified what your priorities are, you cannot be partially committed. A full commitment to what you create is a mandatory catalyst for achieving your team success. By fully understanding your own vision, it will be easier for you to communicate what your vision is to your team. It is highly encouraged to enroll members of your team in your vision by having them understand it as well as or better than you do. Without sharing this knowledge with them, it will be difficult to stay committed to the process and the path you set upon. A significant stumbling block to a unified vision is unforeseeable obstacles in your path that you are not committed to overcoming.

Take the following examples of major companies that failed to properly communicate their vision:

Nokia fell out of step with the market and struggled to turn its good ideas into products. This was caused partly by "*habits of communication that favor unfocused discussions about strategy over clear plans to bring new phone models to market.*"

Enron's collapse can be partially attributed to "*communication-based leader responsibilities*" that senior managers failed to meet. Responsibilities such as "*communicating appropriate values*" and "*maintaining openness to signs of problems.*"

Among the key factors that contributed to the **BP** oil disaster were "*poor communications*" and a failure "*to share important information.*"

The 2012 worldwide **Toyota** recall was a major communications disaster for the firm because it "*forgot the need for transparency.*" Toyota Motors announced that it could face losses totaling as much as $2 billion from lost output and sales worldwide.

Failure to properly communicate slowly chips away at trust between team members. Knowing your priorities, understanding the direction you as an organization are headed, and being honest with yourself about your own truths and myths is a vital foundational element of building and honing a successful team.

CHAPTER 3

STEP TWO—EXAMINE YOUR TEAM

This is a critical aspect of team effectiveness that is too often overlooked. In some cases, poor teamwork results from incorrectly aligning tasks with individuals whose skill sets are not conducive to the assigned task. Reexamine your team members. Really consider what their truths and myths are, just as you authentically did for yourself in step one.

A great way to accomplish this is to spend quality one-on-one time with each member of your team and ask him or her what sort of challenges he or she is facing in the creation of your team's effectiveness. Ask such questions as:

- "Where do you feel you can best contribute to the team's performance?"
- "What about the projects assigned are posing difficulty for you?"

- "Do you know what is expected from you at work?"
- "Do you feel that your opinion counts?"
- "Is there a personal goal you have for yourself that I can help you accomplish?"
- "Do you believe in this company's mission? If not, what would you change about it?"
- "How important is recognition and praise to you for doing good work?"
- "How important is it to you to get updates on your progress?"
- "How often do you need updates to keep you aligned with our mission and purpose?"

It is important to tell your team member at the beginning of your conversation that you will not use his or her responses against him or her and that you are there to help him or her improve. Look for target signs from your team that align you as part of the problem. **Do not respond defensively. Take notes and maintain your composure.**

Gallup's *State of the Global Workplace* report indicated that just 13 percent of employees feel engaged in their jobs. These few are consistently committed to, enthusiastic, and inspired about their roles within an organization.

For as long as I can remember, we have been taught the 80-20 rule, whereby 20 percent of the members that make up an organization carry that organization while the remaining 80 percent ride the wave that the 20 percent create. We are seeing now that this rule is deteriorating in time. What was once 80 percent of people who ride the wave is now 87 percent. This is an increase in "riders" of 8.75 percent. Said another way, this is a decrease in "carriers" and productivity of 35 percent.

The remaining 87 percent are indifferent and unengaged, demonstrate low morale, and work an average of three to five hours a day of an eight-hour schedule. If one of your priorities from step one was to minimize lost production, engaging your team in the vision and mission of your company or organization can have a profound effect on this priority.

Leaders of winning organizations tend to understand that team member engagement drives real production outcomes. These leaders have also incorporated team member engagement as a core value.

Some examples of organizations that have mastered the art of team member engagement are listed below. At the writing of this book, the following companies averaged nine actively engaged employees for every one actively disengaged employee.

- Adventist Health Systems
- CarMax

- DTE Energy
- Hyatt Hotels
- Mars, Incorporated
- Regions Bank
- USAA

TAKE ACTION: Start interviewing your team members now. Make no mention of your disappointment from step one at this stage. Simply state that you are trying to improve overall performance. Save the disappointment talk until the group meeting you will call when you have completed these steps.

CHAPTER 4

STEP THREE—UNDERSTAND YOUR RESPONSIBILITIES: SELF-REFLECTION

Ask yourself, "What role am I personally playing in the motivation and excitement of the team? Are my actions in line with my philosophies and expectations? What has my team said in my interviews with them that aligned me partially with the problem?" If you find you have fallen short of your own and the team's expectations, fess up, take responsibility, and utilize this discovery as the beginning of a new era.

Without self-awareness, you cannot fully understand your truths and myths. Self-awareness allows leaders to project authenticity, demonstrate trustworthiness, have integrity, press on with commitment, and carry the conviction a team needs to stay cohesive and efficient. You represent the organization's mission, but you alone can personify your vision as a leader in the organization. Following are some suggestions to help you "know thyself." When you fully and honestly know yourself, you will be better equipped to evaluate others on your team.

Test yourself. Test yourself by using such personality tests as Myers-Briggs, Predictive Index, and Strength Finder. What you discover will amaze you. Many leaders have a misconception of who they are to themselves and how they appear to others. Oftentimes who they are is at odds with how others see them. Doing such tests as Myers-Briggs and so forth won't make you appear to others differently. But they will shine a light on your own blind spots to help you decide what you choose to do next. The key here is to be open and objective with what you uncover about yourself. Then don't be afraid to choose to change something that you thought was unchangeable.

Be prepared to listen. Listen with your heart. Then qualify with your head. What I mean is: great team leaders see each member of their team as a person, not as human capital. I take issue with the term "human capital" because it dehumanizes the people who make up an organization. By placing them on the same platform as expendable money, the unique qualities of each person are lost in a sea of rapidly arbitraged capital. Unfortunately many team leaders have begun to relate to their members as inanimate, disposable capital. But once you open yourself up to seeing people as human beings and not as capital, you will find them more inspired to put their unique humanity to work for you.

Be sincere. People will know if you are not sincere in your concern for others. When disingenuousness permeates into a team structure, the result is catastrophic. What would have happened to the gallant three hundred Spartans who fought off the Persian army for days if King Leonidas had been insincere with his concern for his soldiers or the reasons why they marched on Thermopylae? The Persian army would have marched unmolested through the mountain pass and likely dominated the Greek city-states before they had a chance to organize a resistance. While the fate of thousands of people living in city-states may not be the outcome of any insincerity with your team, an unpleasant outcome is probable.

Be service-oriented. Do not be taskmaster-oriented. The essence of inspiration occurs when people know that you care about them and their aspirations, not just what they can do for you. Make it a point either once a month or once every few months to move through the organization and seek out random team members. Tell them that you acknowledge their contributions to your team and your goals and that you would like to acknowledge them and their goals.

The message you want to convey is that being on your team is not only about hitting goals and meeting deadlines. It is also about supporting each other inside the workplace and in life. Genuinely seek to be of service to your team members. By helping them achieve their goals while simultaneously achieving yours, you empower each other to do more.

Watch and grade yourself. Set goals, make decisions, and write down what you think will happen. Then after a few months, reevaluate what actually happened with what you thought would. Peter Drucker reintroduced this concept to the public in the *Harvard Business Review* article "Managing Oneself." He writes, "Whenever you make a decision or take a key decision, write down what you expect will happen. Nine or 12 months later, compare the results with what you expected." Feedback analysis is not new, yet many leaders make little or no use of this extremely effective self-reflection tool.

Be aware of others. No one ever did anything amazing on his or her own. Great leaders are able to recognize myths and truths in themselves as well as in their team members. The answer isn't to fire anyone who lacks a strength in a particular role. Rather, the good leader, the strong team leader, will assess his or her personnel in order to better understand their strengths. After such assessment, place each team member in a role that plays to those strengths. The ultimate team leader will go so far as to create a previously non-existent role in order to nurture a unique strength any particular team member may have that was previously underutilized or overlooked.

Here are some guideline questions to help you structure your self-reflection:

- "How am I feeling about that experience/situation?"
- "Why am I feeling this way?"
- "What were my expectations?"
- "Did my experience match my expectations? Why or why not?"
- "What parts of the experience did I have control over?"
- "If I could describe this experience in one to three words, what would those words be?"
- "What actions could I have taken to improve this experience?"
- "What have I learned from this experience?"

The timeless painter, inventor, and engineer Leonardo da Vinci speaks plainly to the importance of self-reflection, "I love those who can smile in trouble, who can gather strength from distress, and grow brave by reflection. 'Tis the business of little minds to shrink, but they whose heart is firm, and whose conscience approves their conduct, will pursue their principles unto death."

Chinese teacher, and politician Confucius explains the place of self-reflection in learning, "By three methods we may learn wisdom: First, by reflection, which is noblest; Second, by imitation, which is easiest; and third by experience, which is the bitterest."

British Philosopher John Locke sums up how self-reflection fits into the repertoire of a gentleman, "Education begins the gentleman, but reading, good company and reflection must finish him."

TAKE ACTION: List the methods by which you will reflect. You may use any or all of the ideas above. Schedule a couple hours a day for the next few days to engage in authentic self-reflection. Consider the self-reflection guideline questions I outlined for you earlier.

CHAPTER 5

STEP FOUR—DISCIPLINARY ACTION

I t is important to reinforce behavior with rewards, but sometimes you need to be ready to drop the hammer if team members are disregarding your expectations and are causing a fissure within the team.

TAKE ACTION: Prepare to notify your team that you will be strictly enforcing a code of discipline for the next three months. Take some time to outline the disciplinary items you will be enforcing. Limit these items to the ones that matter to you the most. It is also worthwhile to consider what the consequences will be for each violation.

When you implement the code and consequences, it is absolutely imperative that you apply disciplinary measures equally to all your team members. You cannot have favorites. Doing so will sever your bond with the rest of your team very quickly. You may lose integrity and trust in a matter of seconds by showing favoritism.

Mention that you will be implementing the "three strikes" rule. Modify this rule, however, to apply to any three violations you find most relevant and important to preserving the culture of your organization. It does not necessarily have to be three recurring strikes on the same infraction. What is very effective is to apply "three strikes" to any action or any combination of three unacceptable actions you will specifically identify above in the **TAKE ACTION** segment of this chapter.

Some ideas for important ground rules to consider are:

- **Tardiness, no more than fifteen minutes late**. Habitually tardy team members are a burden on the rest of the team. If a team member develops the habit of not showing up on time, others must make up for that person's share of the work. They will tire of this very quickly.

- **Missing deadlines**. When a team member or group of team members regularly miss deadlines, they are communicating any combination of the following:

  1. What you asked us to do isn't that important.
  2. The deadline you set was not thought out or was too demanding and unrealistic.

3. We don't trust your judgement for setting deadlines.
4. There are no consequences for disregarding your request.
5. We haven't learned how to work as a team yet.

If reasons 2 and 5 are the cause, look inward, and ask them what about the timeline was either too unrealistic or demanding and what is stopping them from working as a team.

If reasons 1, 3, and 4 are the cause, you will need to have a one-on-one private conversation with the team members who feel that way. Openly discuss with them and try to understand how that mode of thinking developed. Sometimes, discipline is required.

- **Speaking poorly about another team member**. Eleanor Roosevelt said, "Great minds discuss ideas. Average minds discuss events. Small minds discuss people." Allowing gossip erodes trust in a team. If leaders are seen not challenging those who gossip or do not confront those who speak poorly about others, the leader is communicating that he or she agrees with the rumors.

- **Submitting subpar work**. The impact of letting this violation go without consequences is felt in revenues, team morale, cohesiveness, and enthusiasm about the team.

- **Not satisfying expected job requirements**. For example, an accountant should know how to balance budget sheets and read cash flows. If you have team members who cannot satisfy their job requirements, first try re-training, then try re-positioning them in a different role. Lastly, consider replacement. Letting this infraction continue will hurt what you are trying to build.

For each of the infractions above, before you pull out the red pen and record a strike against the team member, try asking him or her if he or she understands the importance of the code he or she violated and why strictly adhering to this code is so important. Ask him or her in the context of how it affects the team, not how it impacts you or how you will look with your bosses, if you have any. If the team member does not understand or has a breakage in learning, teach, retrain, and reward him or her if improvement is shown. If after you have retrained him or her and improvement is not shown, ask the team member once more if he or she does not understand something about what you taught him or her.

An effective way to communicate the importance of adhering to the rules is to ask the team member to repeat what he or she understood to you in his or her own words.

If after you have exhausted these preliminary coaching techniques you see no improvement, you will have to register a first strike against him or her and write up the individual. After you have written him or her up and given him or her the first strike, repeat the coaching for each of the remaining two strikes for any future violations.

Be ready to replace the people in extreme cases. **Identification and enforcement of these infractions must be made constantly and vigilantly for the next three months.** You will weed out the non-committed team members in no time. Once a bad seed is dislodged from the throats of your team, you will find morale and overall productivity much improved.

CHAPTER 6

STEP FIVE—CREATE THE PROCESS FOR MEETING OBJECTIVES

You are the boss. Members of your team will be looking to you for the answers about how to best accomplish their jobs. Even if your team members have natural and raw talent or are well-experienced in their field of work, they will still seek your guidance so as not to disappoint you. At the end of the day, your team members want to make you proud of them. It is up to you to teach, guide, and reward them along the way while enforcing discipline fairly across the board.

Armed with the knowledge that members of your team want to make you happy, help them along by streamlining the process in which they can best accomplish their objectives. Below is an example of a general process flow.

Only assign one person to a task or series of tasks. Do not create and further segment an already fractured team with subteams to accomplish one task. For example, if Sam Smith is very strong in strategy development based on data sets, assign him to take on tasks 6, 8, 9, 13, and 14. See *Figure (5e)* on the next page. Conversely, if Julie Jones loves to investigate and has strong research skills, assign her to tasks 1, 4, 5, 10 in *Figure (5e)* and so forth.

It is usually best to assign your best writer to develop briefs and reviews. This will make it easier to enforce and monitor accountability. If you are the best writer, so be it. Assign yourself to the chore. A chief characteristic for developing effective briefs and reviews is to break down complex information into a simplistic and succinct format. The final version should be simple and concise so as to be easily understood by someone who has no experience or background in the area and who has a very short attention span.

TAKE ACTION: Try to outline something similar to this for a project you currently have pending. Then assign the people who you feel are the best equipped to tackle a specific section of the diagram. Mastering the art of playing to your people's strengths is a rare and powerful skill to build into your leadership style.

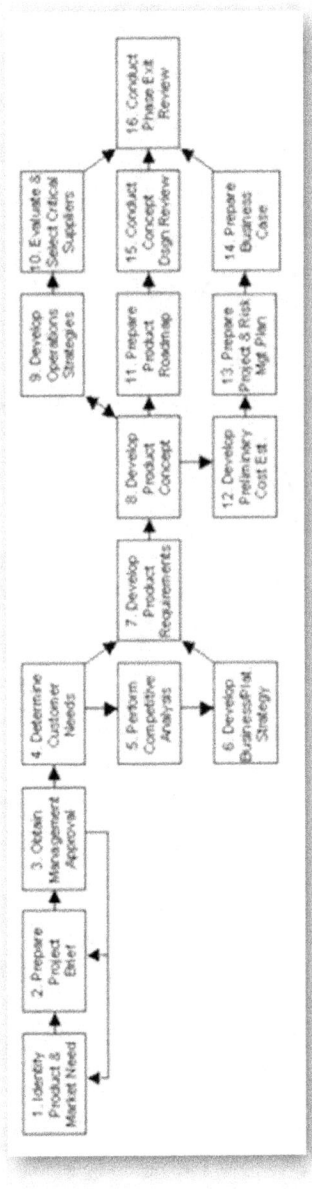

CHAPTER 7

STEP SIX—ASSIGN ACCOUNTABILITY

A ssigning a task to someone is not the same as assigning accountability. Assigning account-ability means holding an individual responsible for the success or failure of a component of the flow process. This person and this person alone will answer for any deficiencies or shortcomings to a specific step in the process. Galvanizing a team into a well-oiled machine starts with you being clear about your expectations. Below are some strategies to help flush out your expectations:

- **SMART Goals**—A great way to foster accountability in the workplace is to set SMART goals for them. SMART goals are goals that are (1) specific, (2) measurable, (3) achievable, (4) results-oriented, and (5) have a time limit or deadline. Having goals that meet these criteria will allow your team members to feel more able in the work they are doing. It is a way for them to measure their own productivity.

- *For example:* Upper management gives the manager of a hotel a mandate to improve occupancy rates in coming months. Improving occupancy rates is too general of a goal. Following the SMART formula, the manager gets more specific. He decides on a goal of 75 percent occupancy per night. The current occupancy rate is 60 percent per night. An increase of 15 percent is a measurable goal. If the hotel improves by 15 percent, the goal was successfully met. The goal is challenging, but a competent manager can certainly achieve it. The goal is results-oriented because it is a challenging one that results in a tangible and empirically verifiable outcome. And finally the goal of improving room occupancy from 60 to 75 percent is to be achieved in ninety days. Now the goal has a time limit, or deadline.

- **Team Incentive Programs**—As I mentioned earlier in this handbook, it is best to motivate your team by reward rather than by discipline. Discipline is to be used as a last resort to enforce and retake order. Leading by reward is also a very effective way to reinforce your commitment to the rest of the team members who want to do well. Not only do team incentive programs give each member an extra dividend for doing his or her job, they provide an environment where team members encourage and support each other to reach a desired result.

- Some incentive programs you can provide to your team members include:

  - **Telecommute hours.** Awarding telecommute hours allows team members to work from home after successfully achieving your goals.

  - **A points program for team members**. Such a program could provide for the redemption of points for a free coffee or lunch nearby. One of my favorite points incentives is awarding points that can be accumulated and redeemed in exchange for paid days off. For example, one hundred points can equal one paid day off.

  - **Team lunches.** It is a simple gesture of appreciation, but scheduling one day where you treat your department or team to lunch, dinner, or drinks for meeting a goal goes a long way in incentivizing people.

  - **Skills courses**. I mentioned earlier in chapter 4, by reaching out to your team and offering to help members reach their goals, you make yourself extraordinary. Be extraordinary and unreasonable in your generosity and commitment to helping your team members reach their individual goals. By offering skills courses as a reward for meeting a goal, you give your team members something they can take with them and keep forever. They will always remember the leader who took the time to serve their needs and propel them toward their aspirations.

- **Production-based bonuses**. For example, in the hotel hypothetical above, a general manager could award a 5 percent quarterly bonus for the line staff or department managers for achieving the 15 percent occupancy increase. This incentive could get expensive. It is best not to lead with it or hold bonuses as a primary incentive.

- **Prioritization**—One reason team member accountability dwindles is because team members may be struggling to balance tasks and goals and can eventually become overwhelmed. When a member of your team gets overwhelmed, it is like the distortion of a link in a chain. If left unaddressed, the link will eventually deteriorate, snapping the entire system you have created. After the first link breaks, the rest follow shortly thereafter. As a leader, in order to mitigate and prevent this possibility, it is important to help your team prioritize their responsibilities in relation to your company's overall goals. By doing so, you will allow them to feel more organized and competent in the tasks they are assigned.

- **Progress Monitoring**—Monitoring your people's progress will motivate them to show you what they are capable of. When I was playing sports and competing in martial arts during my high school and college days, I performed at my best and had my most memorable games and matches when I had the biggest crowds with the most people watching. The members who make up your team are no different. It is only natural that, when we know someone is watching our progress, we will try to perform to our best abilities.

- **Progress Tracking**—It is also important to keep track of the development of your team members. If you see a team member has not shown too much advancement in ninety days in a specific area that can be improved, having a record of his or her progress will play an integral role in structuring the conversation you have with him or her. Try to have progress report meetings once a month with all your key personnel. Every thirty days or so, set aside five to ten minutes with each of them to have an informal, casual conversation of where he or she was some time ago to where he or she is now. If each has shown progress, he or she will be happy to hear it. If he or she has not, he or she will feel that you care about his or her development, appreciate it, and likely show improvement moving forward.

Assigning well-defined deadlines and clearly communicating what outcome you are looking for will greatly enhance your team's comprehension, morale, cohesion, and production. You cannot fault someone for not knowing what he or she is trying to accomplish if you have not set him or her up with that knowledge before judging him or her on it.

While it is imperative to hold team members accountable in their individual roles and performance, it is equally essential to share and spread the credit among the unit, not just between one or two people. Team building is not about you or the individual members of your team. It is about you caring and supporting one another in the pursuit of a unified vision and common direction.

TAKE ACTION: Develop one or two SMART goals to assign to your team.

CHAPTER 8

STEP SEVEN—ESTABLISH A CULTURE OF COMMUNICATION

What is a culture of communication? The Merriam-Webster dictionary defines culture as "*the set of shared attitudes, values, goals, and practices that characterizes an institution or organization… the set of values, conventions, or social practices associated with a particular field, activity, or societal characteristic.*" It then defines communication as "*a process by which information is exchanged between individuals through a common system of symbols, signs, or behavior.*"

When combined, it reads like this, "*The creation of a process by which information is exchanged between individuals through a common system of symbols, signs, or behavior. A process that imparts a set of shared attitudes, values, goals, and practices which characterize an institution or organization in a particular field, activity, or societal characteristic.*"

The culture of communication, said simply, is a way of being by each member of your team:

- That requires little or no forethought;
- By which your team members share and exchange information freely and fluidly with one another;
- That reinforces the team vision, direction, mission, and objective;
- That communicates to an outsider looking in that the identity and values of your team are embedded in who members are and represented instinctively by how they act; and
- That communicates volumes without uttering a single word.

One method I found effective in opening the conversation about developing a culture of communication is to schedule and lead a problem-solving session. This session is not about problems at work. Instead it is about any problems anywhere that is impacting the lives of your team members. The problems they present may be about work, but they may also be about their spouse, child, friend, parent, sibling, dating partner, or any other personal challenge they may be facing. Having this open problem-solving session as the introduction of a culture of communication is a wonderful icebreaker and gets people engaged and comfortable in the structure of sharing with one another.

Moreover, if your colleagues are able to help someone with a problem or challenge he or she is facing outside of work, all will begin to develop a bond of compassion and empathy with each other. It is an extraordinary and unreasonable way to get the momentum going toward establishing a healthy and effective culture of communication.

Other ways to establish a culture of communication are:

- **Daily stand-up meetings**. This is quick, casual, and extremely effective. Every morning before the workday begins, gather everyone around in a standing circle for ten to fifteen minutes and ask if anyone has anything to share. If the answer will consume much of the time allotted here, more than fifteen minutes, thank the person for sharing and ask him or her to schedule a time to see you to discuss your reply further with him or her.

- **Monthly staff meetings**. At least once a month, gather all your department heads around a conference table for a formal one-hour meeting. In turn, your department heads will go through their department's vital statistics. These include such areas as:

  - profit and loss
  - overhead and payroll

- operational excess
- bottlenecks
- employee turnover
- disciplinary issues with their subordinates
- customer issues
- vendor or supplier issues
- their department's standing in relation to each metric you are measuring them on

- **Open-door policy and around-the-clock communication**. Give your team members your cell phone number. Email messages can be misunderstood, misguided, longer than necessary, too short to develop a point, or may get lost in cyberspace and never received. An open-door policy doesn't mean that you can never close your door. It means that your team should feel comfortable approaching you for any problem. It is okay to set a specific time slot per day to *actually have your door open* for anyone to walk in for those so-called "gotta minute" meetings. I discuss "gotta minute" meetings further in chapter 9.

- **Feedback**. Actually encourage your team members to tell you how they think you are doing. If you find them too shy to be truthful with you, ask specifically, "How am I doing?" or "What do you need that I am not providing you?" Another clever way to get feedback is to do anonymous surveys either monthly or quarterly about your specific performance.

- **Project assessments**. Some projects go well; others go badly. Along the way, it is useful to share with your team what is going well or what has gone wrong. As long as you do it in a matter-of-fact, nonaccusatory way, you will find your team emboldened to provide ideas that will help future projects go more smoothly.

- **Informal social outings**. Every once in a while, great leaders take time to relax and enjoy time with their teams. This time is to be free from any work agenda. Work is sure to come up, but communicate to your team that these outings are just to relax and have fun together, not to discuss work unless they want to. Causal activities like bowling, zip-lining, the zoo, lunch, or happy hour create an environment of open candor that isn't present during the regimented workday.

- **State of your team**. Every so often, share a memo or email with your department about how things are going with your direction, mission, and objectives. Be truthful and complete in what you say. If you are falling short of your numbers, share that. Don't point fingers or place blame. Just share it as what it is. If you just hired a new team member, send a brief biography about him or her to the rest of the team. Make sure to copy the new hire on the biography. If you let someone go, share that before rumors spread. Don't say why the person was let go. Just be to the point. "So-and-so was let go. We wish him or her the best." Stop rumors as they spread. Include any other items you find relevant in maintaining your unified vision and providing a culture of open communication.

- **People recognition.** Recognize people for contributions that were tantamount to the team vision. Do not tell others how wonderful these people are when you recognize them. Just point out that a particular action contributed positively to the team objective and that everyone benefitted from that. Do not encourage the 87-13 culture. If one person does a great thing, it is a great thing for the team. Don't make it about any one person. If one person fails the team, do not place blame. Come together to see how you can help as a team.

- **Compassion, openness, and understanding**. Make it a point to assure your teammates that you are there to provide them with the support they need to successfully complete the task you assigned to them. Try to understand if they are having difficulties outside of work. Everyone faces challenges. Congratulate, recognize, and acknowledge people for accomplishments they are proud of. Return focus to the team, but maintain focus on each team member as a vital and important part of the team success. The example in *Figure (7e)* is a situation that every leader will face at some point in his or her career.

Figure (7e)

Problem	Lacey has been distant lately. Her task team has begun complaining to her about her subpar performance. She seems to be disregarding team members' pleas and appears to have an untouchable attitude. Some members of your team bring it to your attention. What do you do?
Answer	Watch Lacey for the next day. If you confirm the reports of her distance and poor performance, take her aside, close your door, and express your concerns. **Don't attack her!** Ask her what has changed over the past three months since you identified her as a rising star.

Result	Lacey breaks down in your office and cries for a few moments before she reveals that she and her husband of nine years are getting divorced and he is seeking custody of the children. *Note here: Despite Lacey's personal matters, she continued to come to work on time and stay late. This says something about Lacey's loyalty and commitment to her team, her job, and you. It cannot be discounted and should be rewarded.*
Solution	Give her three days of paid leave to get her affairs in order. Do not penalize her for these days. Grant them gratis to allow for sick days in the future. Call the gratis days "personal days." Grant early vacation days if you have to. You will find Lacey returned to work with a revitalized attitude and a renewed, even uncompromising, commitment to the team and you especially.

Building a culture of communication sets the tone for every day. And each day, you must reinforce this culture until eventually it will take on a life of its own. In time, you will no longer need to be the catalyst for developing the culture of communication in your organization. What will happen is that the culture you create with your team will nurture growth and common purpose. The culture you create with your team will grow into a way of being that molds the actions of anyone who finds themselves enveloped in its charm. Ultimately this state of harmony will lead to higher levels of performance and better business results.

TAKE ACTION: Create a culture that supports effective team interaction, regardless of position in authority.

CHAPTER 9

STEP EIGHT—EMPOWER INDIVIDUALS, NOT JOB TITLES

Many people hold back their true potential because they feel that, through asserting their skills, they may be violating an existing power structure by performing better than their leader. This outdated idea is called "Outshining the Master." I would, in fact, argue that some contemporary leaders have largely kept this viewpoint alive purposefully in order to hide personal insecurities and self-serving aspirations.

When a leader is fearful of inspiring his or her team members to assert himself or herself powerfully and be the best he or she can be, that leader does not have a team at all. This type of leadership is an autocracy, which has devastating consequences on the team. It is one of the least productive and least effective power pyramids that exist. Autocracy, totalitarianism, dictatorship, and any system of governing where one person holds absolute power suffocates team hegemony, extinguishes would-be flames of brilliance from your people, and wards off individuals who will actually make a difference in the progress of your team and organization in coming months.

To be a powerful leader, one must excel at being a magnanimous servant for one's team. When a leader is not afraid to serve, the team reciprocates in a way that outshines the master in magnanimity. That's awesome! It is a very powerful phenomenon to experience each and every member of your team compete with each other to be more generous, more gracious, more giving of their time, more engaged, more inspired, and more motivated to serve one another. Empower individuals to be the complete, unique, whole, and perfect beings they are. Do not stifle their brilliance.

Tell your team that individual initiative will be rewarded, not seen as a threat to your power. Acknowledge that asking people to shine brilliantly serves the team's objective. Empower them to be better than you are. The truth of the matter is, even if one of your team members has a substantial skill in excess of your own, you will get the credit from the organization for being smart enough to have chosen such a person to be on your team. When you move up in the organization, so will your team members move up with you to fill your vacancy. Everyone wins when you put each other first. So empower them to put each other first.

Below are some ways you can empower your team and develop the culture of service-based leadership:

- **Give up control.** Many leaders I have worked with had a common wrench thrown into their daily productivity. That is, the "gotta minute" conversation that occurs when you are at your desk in your office and one of your team members knocks on your door and asks you if you "gotta minute." The premise by which they ask this question is to help him or her work through a block he or she is experiencing on a project you have assigned. What leaders miss in this exchange however, is that they are being asked so many questions because the individual team members are terrified of acting on their own judgement. They are frightened because a culture of absolute power has been put into place. Oftentimes this fear is mistaken for incompetence. Break that down immediately. They are not incompetent. They are scared. Encourage your team member to put his or her own creativity and individuality into the project. Tell him or her that you believe in his or her own power and you have him or her on your team so he or she can be different than you are, not so he or she can be a duplicate of you. Remind the person that his or her own uniqueness makes them very valuable.

- **Back them up**. Giving up control can be a frightening thought for some leaders. It takes a very confident and worthy leader to have the integrity to give up control and then take responsibility for the outcome. Taking responsibility for the outcome of your team's end product, whether good or bad, is exactly what you have to do in order to build a solid culture and foundation of empowerment. Powerful leaders who sit at the head of powerful teams do not point fingers or pass on blame. They calculate possible outcomes and are prepared to answer for how it all turns out. The leader who is prepared to take responsibility for the good and the bad outcomes will be revered by his or her team and elevated by their superiors.

- **Reward successful outcomes**. Naturally every leader wants his or her team to deliver a successful end product. When this happens, be quick to reward that. Spread the credit among every member who contributed to making it successful.

- **Reward solid effort**. Not every project succeeds. It is okay to have an imperfect record. In all my days consulting for business owners and community leaders, I never met anyone who has a perfect and flawless record. If someone tells me that he or she has never been imperfect and is flawless, I gracefully recuse myself from that assignment and deny my services to him or her. Good effort, however, is not to be overlooked. I am not condoning giving everyone a trophy just for showing up. Far from it. Solid, individual effort from a group of people who gave it their best shot but missed the mark should be recognized and acknowledged. Learn from the imperfections and strive for perfection. Create an environment where the possibility of failure is not to be feared. The likelihood of success should be the fuel that drives the fire that overtakes the possibility of failure.

- **Review existing policies and procedures**. It is unavoidable that red tape and bureaucracy will exist in larger organizations. Smaller organizations too can be the victim of over policy and overregulation. Oftentimes during the growth phase of a smaller organization, stringent policies and procedures are put into place to stay the course, as they say. Over time the policies that were helpful at one time can become no longer valuable. In fact, the very same policies that were effective in the past may turn into the culprits that prevent fruitful team development. Once in a while, review the policies and procedures of your organization. If the reason they were created in the first place no longer exists, get rid of them. Your organization should be able to adapt to changing environments. By reviewing antiquated policies and procedures and doing away with them, you will contribute remarkably to team success.

When your team members know it is okay to be themselves and will receive credit for everyone doing well, motivation becomes less of a problem. You will find your team members encouraging and motivating each other to do better and reach higher.

TAKE ACTION: Review your organization's policies and procedures, and do away with disadvantageous and excessive regulation.

CHAPTER 10

STEP NINE—RESOLVE CONFLICTS THAT ARISE

A colossal barrier to effective teamwork is mistrust among team members. Therefore one highly effective technique you can apply to resolving team conflict is a face-to-face he-said-she-said discussion. If there is friction among any members of your team, rather than speak with each person separately, call both into your office and serve as the mediator to resolve the conflict in the team's best interest.

Once your team members realize they can trust you to resolve their problems and you will not take sides, they will return to work more trusting, open, and willing to share their knowledge with another. More importantly, you will find them more eager to share the credit for a job well done.

Your team will respect your involvement and will reenter the project with renewed appreciation for your leadership of the team.

Below is an overview of how to conduct the face-to-face conflict resolution session. Take off your boss hat, and put on your objective, neutral, and impartial mediator hat.

- **Do not take sides**. It is vital that you do not take sides or even give the impression that you are. Once one party feels you are taking sides, he or she will quickly shut down, and the possibility of reaching a compromise ends with it. To avoid taking sides and the impression of doing so, mind your body language, monitor your demeanor, avoid agreeing with one party over another, and ask probative and clarifying questions. Refrain from asking investigative questions that look for fault.

- **Mind your body language**. Maintain eye contact. <u>Do not</u> nod in agreement. <u>Do</u> say such encouraging statements as "go on" or "tell me about that." Avoid saying things like "I agree" or "You make a valid point." Take notes. Keep your legs uncrossed and your pen moving. Position your upper body toward both parties in an open and receptive manner.

- **Pay attention to your demeanor**. Do not slouch or sit at the edge of your chair. Speak with an impartial tone, and avoid inflections in your voice that show favor to one party over another.

- **Ask probative questions; do not look for who is at fault**. Probative questions are inquiries that draw out the facts. A common difficulty leaders encounter when dealing with conflict occurs when the focus of the conversation is on - or shifts to - perception and feeling rather than on the facts as they actually happened. Avoid directing the conversation to who perceived what and how that made him or her feel. Opinions are not a valid measure of what actually transpired. Focus on drawing out the facts because it is the facts that are in dispute. Moreover, it is easier to reconcile facts than people's opinions. Once you are able to do away with the story each party is telling you about what happened, you can redirect the conversation to what actually happened. If one party mentions a third party as a witness or as a coconspirator, halt the conversation, and call the third party into the room with you. Discontinue your conflict resolution session, and sit quietly until the third party arrives. When the third party arrives, ask him or her probative questions. If the third party is a substantial contributor to the events, ask him or her to grab a seat and include him or her as a separate and detached party to the conflict for the rest of the mediation.

- **Ask clarifying questions**. Rephrase what the other person is saying so you make sure you are listening correctly. A powerful tool I have used to better understand another person's point of view is to rephrase what someone tells me in my own words and ask if that is what he or she meant. It is easy to assign incorrect meaning to what someone is actually telling you. Avoid assigning your unique meaning of words to another person's point of view. Ask clarifying questions along the way so you make sure you understand what is being said. By the same token, the speaker will feel more comfortable opening up to you because he or she knows you are hearing what he or she is saying.

- **When tempers flare**. Sometimes tempers mount. When this happens, ask the more level-headed party to leave the room for a moment while you speak with the emotional party alone. Once you have calmed the emotional party by focusing your conversation on the facts, ask him or her to wait outside for a moment while you speak with the awaiting party alone. This practice defuses the tensions for the moment and allows you to finish extrapolating facts without emotional interruption that may not be factual at all.

- **Help them find common ground**. Search for ground everyone can agree on and build a new ground all can stand on together. Focus the conversation on what each person's interests really are. Do not focus the discussion on who did what. When team members engage in conflict, the heart of the issue is competing interests, not the actions of the combatants. It is important to know who did what, but a skillful mediator will refocus the conversation on what each party wants. By understanding what each party wants, the mediator can steer the conversation into a direction where tensions simmer down, possibilities arise, and competing interests find a cooperative foundation. A good question to ask is, "What about that has gotten you angry?"

TAKE ACTION: In all your conversations for the next thirty days, practice asking probative questions and making clarifying inquiries. Remain objective, impartial, and neutral while focusing on drawing out facts and filtering out opinions.

CHAPTER 11

STEP TEN—CALL THE "CHANGE MEETING"

Now that you have successfully studied and resolved to answer the above questions and outlined the direction you want to take your team, call the "Change Meeting," a mandatory meeting where you communicate your expectations and your philosophy. It is a good time to recognize and appreciate individual members of your team. A powerful practice when recognizing people is to recognize them as unique and powerful people with unique strengths. Highlight those strengths, not how they do their work better than someone else.

Example 1. Susie is a top performer. She is a good, consistent, and reliable worker. She is also a great listener and terrific speaker. Highlight her strengths. Acknowledge her for that great presentation she gave the other day and how well she received criticism and feedback from the audience.

Example 2. John is not a top performer, but he has been with the organization a long time. He knows a lot of the history of the institution you represent and has known many of the leaders who came before you. Acknowledge his tenure, and share with the team a part of the history of the firm he shared with you. Let him know that what he does know is valuable to the team, even if he is not a top performer.

Sometimes, in the example of John above, many Johns end up being top performers because you inspired them by acknowledging you appreciate them as unique and special individuals.

Now is also a good opportunity to share the following:

- You are committed to helping them achieve their career and personal goals.

- You will be having individual, private, confidential conversations with everyone over the next few days. Remind them to be candid and open and no disciplinary action or retaliation will come from these conversations.

- You do not expect perfection, and it is okay to fail. Failure is okay so long as everyone is authentically doing his or her very best to contribute to the team.

- You will hold individuals accountable and measure success by team accomplishment.

- Tell them they are empowered to be themselves. They are each unique, whole, complete, and perfect. Explain how you will take responsibility for an imperfect end product and how you will distribute the credit for a successful end product among the team.

- Explain that you will be phasing out the "gotta minute" conversation to further their empowerment.

- Introduce the new structure of meetings such as formal monthly meetings for all key department heads and informal daily stand-up meetings for everyone.

- Lay the ground rules and share how discipline will work.

- Explain the "three strikes" rule from chapter 5.

In some states, this mandatory meeting must be paid even if attendees do not do any physical work. Please check with your local labor department to determine the regulation on this issue.

Have a list of positive comments to say about each member of the team. Highlight these positive attributes and share them with everyone when you start the meeting. The key is to start on a positive note. It is crucial to maintain an encouraging and optimistic tone throughout the three hours you spend communicating your findings from these steps.

Even when you are talking about the deficiencies plaguing the current system, speak about how your combined contributions will reverse the negatives. Make the session interactive; don't just talk at the team.

Make sure to announce that this change is in everyone's best interest and a lack of change will result in difficult situations for everyone on the team, perhaps even job loss. Maintain a watchful eye for those who appear to be clearly engaged and for others who are only there because it is a mandatory meeting.

TAKE ACTION: Schedule the "Change Meeting." It should take approximately three hours. It is a good idea to supply finger food, coffee and snacks.

CHAPTER 12

STEP ELEVEN—WATCH LIKE A HAWK

The next three weeks after the meeting are crucial to the solidification of your high-powered team. Here, you identify the weakest links and try to help them. If team members are unable to grasp their responsibilities or fail to execute to your standards, move them to a different position in your organization that utilizes their strengths. Observe them for thirty days in their new role. Watch for any productivity increases from this move. Embolden your team members to continue improving where you have already seen improvement.

TAKE ACTION: Keep an especially watchful eye on your superstars to confirm your impression of their abilities. With the same urgency, keep a watchful eye for strengths of your team members who have been hidden away by these individuals by being assigned to a role that is incompatible with their strengths. Move these team members to a more constructive position.

Here are some best practices tips for watching team member performance:

- **Create a base criteria for performance standard**. The base criteria is the minimum required performance standard you expect from every member of your team. For example, have a maximum number of allowable tardy infractions of fifteen minutes or more over a fifty-two-week span. Another example is to set forth a basic standard for the treatment of fellow team members. If a member of your team is regularly complained about as abrasive, hostile, or disrespectful, it needs to be addressed through the base criteria for performance standard. By setting respect toward one another as a base criteria for performance, you will have implemented a proactive way of being that prevents such occurrences from ever happening.

- **Spend less time in your office**. Get out of your office from time to time, stretch, and check in with your people. The surest way to watch team member performance is to physically watch team member performance with your own eyes. Walk out of your office without a specific team member in mind. Stop by a random workspace, say hello, and ask how he or she is doing. Then ask if he or she needs anything for the project you assigned or in his or her personal life. If he or she needs anything, provide it for him or her. If not, ask the team member how the task you assigned is coming along. Spending less time in your office and interacting with your people lets them know that you care about them and you are watching them. By asking if they need anything, not only are you helping your team members, you are also proactively putting out fires before they burn the rest of the team.

- **Be specific when asking for commitments and then hold everyone accountable for their word.** Everyone struggles with keeping their word to themselves and others 100 percent of the time. I do not know anyone who has a perfect promise-keeping record. And that is okay. It is not wrong. Life happens. People get it. If one can keep his or her word at least a majority of the time, productivity increases exponentially. Hold people accountable for their promises. Remind them that keeping their integrity on what they declare they will do is essential to creating a workable, reliable, and pleasant work experience. When you hold people accountable for their promises, integrity will consistently permeate into their personal life. Being able to make a declaration and have people believe the declaration will in fact come to pass is a very powerful way of being. It transforms every aspect of life. By holding people to their word, you positively impact team performance and help your team members be powerful in their personal life. As the leader, you must lead by example and keep your word the most.

- **Request a daily or weekly memo**. Request a daily or weekly memo from your key personnel. The memo should contain declared goals and progress in relation to those objectives. It does not have to be long or excessive. It does not have to describe all the goals that are, in fact, in action. Focusing the memo report from your key personnel to one or two tangible and quantifiable goals per week is sufficient.

- **Watch for negative attitudes**. A team member who does not seem motivated and inspired by the work he or she is doing is experiencing a block in terms of fully appreciating his or her role on the team. He or she is also harming everyone who is relying on them. Behavioral signs by a team member that indicate negative attitudes are forming include regularly coming to work late, keeping to themselves, spreading rumors, unwelcoming body language, leaving early, and rarely staying late. When you see this occurring on your team with one or any number of team members, it must be addressed. One poisonous seed can infect an entire population. Even if other team members had positive attitudes, regular exposure to someone with a negative disposition will either spread the negativity or force your top performers away from your team to avoid the drama. In some cases, a bad attitude can be triggered by job or personal insecurity or just a sincere dislike for the work being done. In any case, you as the leader need to get to the bottom of it. Watch closely for negative attitude patterns, and proactively be in action to fix them.

CHAPTER 13

STEP TWELVE—LEAD BY EXAMPLE

G ood leaders inspire others to be the best they can be. Great leaders inspire others by being who they want others to be. Leading by example is contagious.

When leaders say one thing and do something else or hold others to a higher standard than they hold themselves, they lose confidence and trust among their team members. Here are some ways you can avoid the peril of eroding confidence:

- **Commit to everyone's success**. The success of those who follow you measures your success. Commit to the success of every individual on your team. After all, you hired them, and you once saw their potential. Get it back out of them.
- **Be truthful**. Show that honesty is the best policy and integrity is never for sale.

- **Share knowledge; be a teacher first**. Freely share your knowledge and teach before you scold. Try to retrain your people at least three times before you take disciplinary action.
- **Be fair across the board and consistently enforce**. Enforce your strict code of discipline. Make no exceptions because, if you do, you will lose the mystique of the new era legitimacy. Treat everyone the same way. Hold everyone to the same basic standards.
- **Be in a state of constant evolution**. Be aware of changing technology or methods that can speed up the projects you are working on.
- **Listen.** Your team members may come up with great ideas to improve your workflow and work process. Take some time to hear your people out. By listening to ideas, you improve morale and boost creativity.
- **Maintain "innocent until proven guilty."** Respect everyone as a positive contributor until he or she proves otherwise.
- **Resolve conflict quickly and expertly**. Handle power and politics carefully. Use the conflict resolution method from step nine.
- **Strive to be the perfection you are asking from your team**. Do your job as well as you possibly can, admit to any mistakes you made, and be in action to fix it.

Here are several leaders who are well known for leading by example:

Jim Sinegal, former CEO of Costco: Under his leadership, Costco's stock doubled, and revenues grew at an impressive rate. Sinegal paid himself a yearly salary of $350,000 because he figured he shouldn't be paid more than twelve people working on the floor. His employee turnover rate was the lowest in the retail industry, over *five times less* than rival Walmart.

Nelson Mandela: A tribal king, Chief Jongintaba, adopted Nelson Mandela. Mandela credits Chief Jongintaba as a major source of leadership learning. Chief Jongintaba would frequently hold meetings of the court. Men would gather in a circle and express their opinion. The chief waited until everyone had spoken before he would enter the conversation. Mandela would later use his father's technique, gathering leaders at his kitchen table or in his driveway and hold discussions. Mandela would always listen first and speak last.

Muhammad Ibn Abdallah Ibn Abd Almuttalib Ibn Hashim: Also known as the Prophet Muhammad in the Muslim world, he was one of the greatest leaders of all time. Muhammad led the spread of Islam in and around Arabia. He united a chaotic society in the name of morality and humanity and led his people out of severe persecution and mistreatment. In fact, there is an entire segment of learning in Islam that teaches Muslims how to act by following his example. It is a learning in and of itself called *Hadith* and extends beyond the teachings of the Qur'an. Islam is the second-largest and the fastest-growing religion of the world today.

Steve Jobs: Steve Jobs was the cofounder of Apple with Steve Wozniak. After being fired from Apple he went on to create companies NeXT and Pixar. Apple ultimately bought NeXT, and Jobs found himself back at Apple. Jobs believed in nothing less than excellence from everyone he worked with. He summed up his observations succinctly when he said, "Be a yardstick of quality. Some people aren't used to an environment where excellence is expected."

TAKE ACTION: Take one hour a day for the next week and evaluate yourself sincerely. Are there areas in your leadership where you are asking for something from others that you are not willing to do yourself? Are you being fair? Are you being truthful?

CHAPTER 14

Step Thirteen - Trust

The truth of the matter is that we learn to trust only by repeatedly taking personal risk and experiencing positive outcomes. As I mentioned earlier, trust is earned. It's not automatic and cannot be imposed. Interpersonal trust can be viewed as having five components:

- **Truth**. Be transparent with your team. Be honest, and be genuine.

- **Respect**. A respectful workplace provides a host of benefits for you and your team. Respect in the workplace improves working relationships, reduces stress, decreases conflict, and boosts productivity.

- **Understanding**. In his famous work *7 Habits of Highly Effective People*, Stephen R. Covey reminds us to "seek first to understand then to be understood." True understanding is seeing what someone is saying from his or her point of view, not ours. When we do the opposite, that is, seek to be understood first and listen from our point of view, the other person feels ignored completely. Eventually he or she will just shut down and become a silent part of your team. Part of establishing team success is to inspire others to be active, vocal, creative partners of your team. When you shut people out, they no longer become partners in the bigger picture, and a vital element of team success is compromised.

- **Support**. Provide your team members with everything they need to be successful on your team and in their personal life.

- **Integrity**. Declare what you will do, and do what you have declared.

Some exercises to build trust with relative ease and low cost are:

- Limited Senses
- Traffic Jam
- All Aboard
- Who's Got the Dollar?
- Trust Walk

Limited Senses: Create a clear space in a large area with adequate safety precautions. I like to have several participants or co-facilitators act as buffers. Give each participant a number, instruct him or her not to share it with anyone, and then blindfold each participant. Tell everyone that no one is allowed to talk. The goal is to put themselves in numeric order without seeing or talking. The real interesting part is that you do not give the participants consecutive numbers. Skip around with little regard to the pattern, for example, 1, 2, 3, 5, 8, 9, 10, 14, 17, and 18. You should always have a one and the number that represents the number of participants in the activity.

Traffic Jam: There are seven stepping-stones and six people. On the three left-hand stones, facing the center, stand three of the people. The other three people stand on the three right-hand stones, also facing the center. The center stone is not occupied. Everyone must move so the people originally standing on the right-hand stepping-stones are on the left-hand stones, and those originally standing on the left-hand stepping-stones are on the right-hand stones, with the center stone again unoccupied.

Restrictions:

a) After each move, each person must be standing on a stepping-stone.

b) If you start on the left, you may only move to the right. If you start on the right, you may only move to the left.

c) You may "jump" another person if there is an empty stone on the other side. You may not "jump" more than one person.

d) Only one person can move at a time.

All Aboard: The object of the game is to get all of the people in the group onto the board. You can either use a poster board, wood board, or whatever board works best. Everyone must have at least one foot on the board. HINT: Try not to give solutions, but tell everyone to listen to others' ideas. You may enlarge or decrease the size of the board, depending on the degree of challenge you would like.

Who's Got a Dollar: This is a good initial exercise for newly forming team members. The leader stands up and asks the team, "Who's got a dollar?" And waits patiently. Eventually someone comes up with a dollar bill. The leader walks over to the giver and asks for the dollar. While holding the bill together with the giver, asks the giver, "What are your hopes and aspirations for this company or organization?" When the giver has answered the question, the leader takes the dollar from the giver and walks over to another person, handing someone else the giver's dollar. The leader asks the recipient the same question, and listens to his or her answer. Next the leader asks the group, "Who's got a ten-dollar bill?" The same question is asked of the giver and then of the recipient of the ten-dollar bill. Now the leader asks, "Who's got a twenty-dollar bill?" Again the question is asked, and a transfer of money takes place. At this point, the leader stops, asks for the money to be returned to its rightful owners, and explains the importance of trust to the performance of teams. The leader asks each person to silently reflect on his or her thoughts and feelings about trusting one another that the money would be returned while the exercise was in progress. Ask those who didn't volunteer why they did not.

Trust Walk: Find a good location with some obstacles but nothing dangerous. Some good locations may include the woods or a large field. Form pairs. Ask one partner to be the navigator (guide) and the other to be blindfolded. When the blindfolded partner is ready, slowly spin the person around a few times so he or she does not know which direction he or she is headed. From this point on, the guide should not touch the partner at all, but rely solely on verbal cues. (For example, "About five steps ahead, there is a branch. Step over it slowly.") The guide is solely responsible for his or her partner's safety. He or she should navigate to avoid obstacles.

TAKE ACTION: Delegate an important task to someone on your team. Give them the objective and tell them to take ownership of it. Empower him or her

to put their own unique creativity and style into it. Be hands off, but ask for weekly updates. Encourage the free flow of thoughts and ideas.

CHAPTER 15

STEP FOURTEEN—NEVER GIVE UP

At times, turning around team performance, especially with larger-sized teams, can be a daunting challenge. However, the worst thing you can do is stop partway through the change program and not follow up or follow through.

Perseverance, like leading by example, is contagious. When team members sense your unwavering commitment and dedication to their success, they will help you along the way. With their help, the daunting challenge will gradually become easier and more rewarding.

Examples of leaders who faced hard times fills history. Through the help of their teams, however, they were able to reach unprecedented success. We saw the example of Steve Jobs earlier with his termination and eventual rehire to Apple. Consider the following leaders who overcame tumultuous times and achieved historic results:

Abraham Lincoln: Widely held as the American president who saved the Union from itself, he is the only reason that the nation did not break into smaller parts. Slavery was ended under his presidency when he signed the Emancipation Proclamation.

Bill Gates: He once had a company called Traf-O-Data. He and partner Paul Allen created a device that was supposed to read traffic tapes and process the data. The device was meant to optimize traffic and end road congestion. They first tried to sell the processing service to the local county, but their demo failed because the machine didn't work. Gates later recalls that his challenges with Traf-O-Data were "seminal in preparing us to make Microsoft's first product a couple of years later."

Thomas Edison: Thomas Edison failed ten thousand times before creating the lightbulb. His response to repeated attempts that did not work was, "I have not failed. I've just found ten thousand ways that won't work."

Sir Richard Branson: Branson had poor reading and math skills and dropped out of high school. He is proud to admit he has been dyslexic all his life. Once upon a time, his Virgin record shops faced cash flow problems. Other ventures the billionaire entrepreneur did not find much luck with included Virgin Cola, Virgin Vodka, Virgin Vie, Virgin Brides, Virgin Clothing, Virgin Cars, and Virgin Digital. Branson imparts this wisdom to would-be leaders and entrepreneurs, "Learn from failure. If you are an entrepreneur and your first venture wasn't a success, welcome to the club!"

Vincent van Gogh: Van Gogh only sold **one painting** during his lifetime, the "Red Vineyard at Arles." This painting now resides at the Pushkin Museum in Moscow. The rest of van Gogh's more than nine hundred paintings were not sold or made famous until after his death.

You don't have to die before you receive the validation you are working toward. Nor do you have to be a president during wartime or a billionaire entrepreneur to know that failure is a part of success. You simply need to believe in yourself and your team. Give each project your best effort. Treat each member of your team with care and respect. Move together in synchronized harmony with a clear purpose, vision, and direction in mind. And never give up. The rest will come together in time.

TAKE ACTION: If you are thinking of giving up, don't!

CHAPTER 16

STEP FIFTEEN—CELEBRATE YOUR SUCCESS

You have just completed a difficult project. Management is pleased, and your customers are thrilled. Your team did an outstanding job. Now is the time to thank the people who made it happen. A two-minute speech at the end of the day telling everyone what a great job they did is not enough. Plan a celebration that goes beyond a pat on the back.

Consider that your team did not do a halfway job in completing a successful project. You should not do a halfway job in acknowledging team members for a job well done.

- **Decide how you will celebrate**. In putting together your celebration, make the decision of what you will do based on your team. Ask what everyone will enjoy. What will make this time together different from the usual happy hour "thanks" outing? The objective of your celebration is to make everyone on the team feel remembered and valued.

- **Publicly declare a celebration**. In the declaration of celebration, announce how proud you are of your team. Send an email or post a memo to senior managers and invite them. It may be a good idea to invite your customers as well. Even if they don't attend, your team will appreciate the fact that you announced their success to the higher-ups and to those who they are in business to serve, the customer or client.

- **Name names**. In your memo of intent to celebrate, acknowledge each member of your team by his or her name. Say a sentence about how each contributed to the success of the project. It is not enough to offer a blanket "thank you" to your team. Go the extra mile and recognize everyone for his or her contributions to the success of the project. Let everyone know that you have been watching for ways to reward, not for ways to reprimand.

- **Pay close attention**. Take time to talk to everyone at the celebration. Ask what each person found helpful and what he or she found challenging. Ask each individual what he or she learned from this experience. And ask all to tell you a little bit about how he or she has grown from the project. You can learn a great deal by taking this opportunity to talk to your people.

Finally, enjoy your success. Don't forget to take this time to do some reflection of your own. Think back to the challenges you faced, how you felt when facing them, and what you did to find the solution. Explore within yourself how you have grown from this experience. Don't do any work when you get home. Relax, enjoy your family and friends, and take a well-deserved rest. You've earned it.

TAKE ACTION: Plan your celebration party! Enjoy a job well done and relax.

NOTES

NOTES

NOTES

NOTES

References

"Most Small-Business Failures Tied to Poor Management." Accessed March 14, 2017. http://www.bizjournals.com/portland/stories/2000/04/10/smallb4.html.

"10 Reasons Why Strategic Plans Fail." Accessed March 14, 2017. https://www.forbes.com/sites/aileron/2011/11/30/10-reasons-why-strategic-plans-fail/#5a851686a8ba.

"A Failure to Communicate." Accessed March 14, 2017. https://www.trainingjournal.com/articles/feature/failure-communicate.

"40 Organizations Leading the World in Employee Engagement." Accessed March 14, 2017. http://www.gallup.com/opinion/gallup/182432/organizations-lead-world-employee-engagement.aspx.

"How Leaders Become Self-Aware." Accessed March 14, 2017. https://hbr.org/2012/07/how-leaders-become-self-aware.

"Self-Reflection: Leading by Taking Time to Know Ourselves." Accessed March 14, 2017. http://msue.anr.msu.edu/news/self_reflection_leading_by_taking_time_to_know_ourselves.

"Reflection Quotes." Accessed March 14, 2017. https://www.brainyquote.com/quotes/keywords/reflection.html.

"Talking about Others: The Good, the Great and the Intolerable." Accessed March 16, 2017. https://www.forbes.com/sites/davidkwilliams/2013/12/27/talking-about-others-the-good-the-great-and-the-intolerable/#520c4a05f45a.

"Employee Accountability in the Workplace." Accessed March 16, 2017. https://timewellscheduled.com/employee-accountability-in-the-workplace.

"8 Best Employee Incentive Programs." Accessed March 16, 2017. https://www.goco.io/blog/8-best-employee-incentive-programs.

"10 Ways to Create a Culture of Open Communication." Accessed March 16, 2017. http://www8.gsb.columbia.edu/articles/node/1746/10-ways-to-create-a-culture-of-open-communication.

"10 Tips on How to Empower and Engage Your Employees." Accessed March 24, 2017. http://www.talentculture.com/10-tips-on-how-to-empower-and-engage-your-employees.

"Body Language and Demeanor—Body Language." Accessed March 24, 2017. http://careers.stateuniversity.com/pages/100000462/Body-Language-Demeanor-Body-Language.html.

"How to Observe Employee Performance." Accessed March 24, 2017. http://smallbusiness.chron.com/observe-employee-performance-19393.html.

"5 Factors That Affect Your Employee's Productivity." Accessed March 27, 2017. https://www.nbrii.com/employee-survey-white-papers/5-factors-that-affect-your-employees-productivity.

"Negative Attitudes That Affect Businesses." Accessed March 27, 2017. http://smallbusiness.chron.com/negative-attitudes-affect-businesses-21662.html.

"Top 10 Ways to Lead by Example." Accessed March 28, 2017. http://www.soulcraft.co/essays/lead_by_example.html.

"10 Business Leaders You Should Strive to Emulate." Accessed March 28, 2017. http://www.businessinsider.com/10-examples-of-excellent-business-leadership-2010-2/how-southwest-handled-911-1#how-nelson-mandelas-father-made-tribal-decisions-7.

"Leadership and 10 Great Leaders from History." Accessed March 28, 2017. https://www.industryleadersmagazine.com/leadership-and-10-great-leaders-from-history.

"The Innovator Steve Jobs." Accessed March 28, 2017. http://www.leadershiplime.com/innovator-steve-jobs.html.

"Why Is Respect So Important in the Workplace?" Accessed March 28, 2017. http://content.wisestep.com/respect-important-workplace.

"The 7 Habits of Highly Effective People, Habit 5: Seek First to Understand, Then to Be Understood." Accessed March 28, 2017. https://www.stephencovey.com/7habits/7habits-habit5.php.

"Failure Is Feedback: How 5 Billionaires Had to Fail to Succeed." Accessed March 28, 2017. http://www.hongkiat.com/blog/fail-to-succeed-billionaires.

"16 Wildly Successful People Who Overcame Huge Obstacles to Get There." Accessed March 28, 2017. http://www.huffingtonpost.com/2013/09/25/successful-people-obstacles_n_3964459.html.

"How to Celebrate Team Success." Accessed March 28, 2017. http://www.techrepublic.com/article/how-to-celebrate-team-success.